RESEARCH IN ISLAM

BASICS, PRINCIPLES AND
PRACTICAL SUGGESTIONS

AHMAD VON DENFFER

The Islamic Foundation

© The Islamic Foundation, 1983/1403 AH

Reprinted 1985
ISBN 0 86037 133 6

Published by:

The Islamic Foundation
223 London Road
Leicester, UK

Quran House
P. O. Box 30611 Nairobi, Kenya

PMB 3193 Kano, Nigeria

British Library Cataloguing in Publication Data
Denffer, Ahmad von
    Research in Islam
    1. Islam
    I. Title
    297   B161.2
    ISBN 0-86037-133-6

Printed and bound in Great Britain by
Dotesios (Printers) Ltd
Bradford-on-Avon, Wiltshire.

CONTENTS

SECTION I

SOME BASICS OF RESEARCH WORK

BASICS OF RESEARCH

First a note about the technique of this book. I will give you a few formulas, which may initially look like some kind of chemistry, but they are not. They are abbreviations of principles and methods and it is helpful to learn and to apply them.

PRINCIPLE Q (question)

The first principle in research is 'Q', i.e. the abbreviation for *question* because the first step in any research work is *asking questions*.

If your mind is not willing or not awake or too lazy to ask questions you will never be able to do research work. If you just absorb what you hear or what you read but never challenge it and do not question the information you receive, then you will fail to reach your goal. This is the first principle: critical thinking and questioning constitute the basis of any research. As far as research in Islam is concerned, the formula is Q(2), which means asking questions about the Qur'an. That is the basis of any Islamic research and we shall discuss it later.

MEANING OF RESEARCH

What do we imagine a person who does research to look like? Will he wear glasses, have a frowned forehead and white hair? Perhaps we can discern that he looks intelligent and also somewhat worried because of the heavy burden on his shoulders? Appearance may of course deceive. You must be very clear about the *meaning* of things and not be deceived by their outer appearances. When you hear that someone is doing research, this in the first instance does not mean much at all - it is just a label. Apply the principle Q; the first *question* you have to ask is: what is he *actually doing?* Do not be satisfied by the general statement that he is doing research. What *kind* of research is he doing?

Think of the meaning of research. Search means of course to look for something, and in the word research the word search has been combined with the Latin syllable 're'. 'Re' means to do something again and again, like re/arrangê, re/fit, etc. Research means simply: *to look in detail or to search intensively*.

Of course 'research', when employed in technical language, means *fact-finding*, for the purpose of presenting facts in some way, be it in description, in analysis, in formulating a theory, or any other way.

KINDS OF RESEARCH

The research discussed in this handbook can be subdivided into three kinds:

One kind of research is factual, concerned with the mere facts. For example, we may wish to know what percentage of the population in this country are Muslims? We would have to find some sources, and by tapping these sources obtain the required information.

Another kind is historical research. For example, we may want to know how the British were able to gain a foothold in Malaysia and how they were able to transform the whole society in a period of 200 years. One needs to be specially careful with historical research. History has usually been written by people belonging to the dominating or ruling group. Almost all of the history of Malaysia has been written by officers from the British colonial Administration. Whatever they perceived may be something entirely different from what we want to know. One needs to be aware of the possibility of bias in sources.

A third kind of research is background research. If, for example, we wish to describe the pre-history of the Islamic revolution in Iran, we ask: how was it possible that in that particular situation in the late 1970s 'suddenly' the Shah was thrown out of the country and a whole new political and social process was initiated? Here we need to know the background and hence we would do background research, which is a combination of factual and historical research.

Field Research and Library Research

There are two basic 'locations' for research: 'outside' and 'inside'. 'Outside' research is what we call 'fieldwork'. Field research deals with real life, while library research deals with whatever has already been collected by field researchers. They have put it into writing, on paper, into books and other information storage systems and we work on this basis whereas when we do field research we go outside and collect information ourselves.

There are a number of issues that need to be observed. However we shall not be much concerned with field research in this initial stage, and hence it will only be discussed briefly.

Field research is the more difficult part of research work and it may not be suitable for beginners. The relationship between a researcher and the people he meets is of great importance and there are many aspects which you need to be aware of. You may want to do research in Wales where the people speak Welsh and if you do not know the language you will need somebody to interpret for you. This person serves like a filter, he will change whatever you ask into his own words and the meaning to some extent will also change. What he is told he will translate for you and it will once more be influenced by him. This is a kind of filter which you need to be aware of when you rely on interpretation.

Again, when you go somewhere to ask questions in order to find out things, people will form certain ideas about you. They will react to you in accordance to their perception of you. If they like you they may readily give the information that you require, but if they do not like you they will be reluctant to help you. They may smile at you and say: 'Yes, indeed, it is exactly the way you say it is', while in fact it is not.

Lastly, you should be aware that field research is not always necessary. If the library contains the required data there is no real need for you to go out into the field.

Library Research, on the other hand, seems more easy. Although we are dealing as much with real life, as in field research, we do not deal with real people but with the printed word. Once things have been written down and printed they do not change any more. They are no longer flexible. What we have to critically evaluate is their pre-history, before they were written down, and our own way of receiving them and reacting to them. We need to ask many questions concerning this but once something is in writing it does not change.

For library research we have a variety of materials we can utilise. Firstly, there are different kinds of printed sources. These begin with *handbooks, guides* and basic *introductions* to a topic. For example, you will find many books written as a basic introduction to Islam. Then there are *reference books* and *encyclopaedias* like the Encyclopaedia Britannica, or the Encyclopaedia of Islam, which was produced by a large team of Orientalists, etc.

Most important in the beginning are *bibliographies*. A bibliography is a list of books in which the author, name and place of the publisher and the date of a publication are mentioned. There are numerous bibliographies on each and every subject. One specially recommended is included in this volume: A.R. Siddiqui, *Islamic Studies: A Select Guide to Bibliographic and Reference Material*. It lists some basic books which anyone would need to refer to for general knowledge as well as for beginning in Islamic studies. It contains information on reference books, encyclopaedias, etc. It helps you to know what books are available and from where to start.

Then there is a very important source which is often overlooked: *dissertations and theses*. Usually dissertations and theses are not printed in large numbers. Many are just photocopied and a few copies bound. A few copies remain in the university where the degree was taken, and a few are sent to other libraries. At the most about 20-25 copies exist of a single title, but often they contain very important information. *Bibliographies* of dissertations are available and you should consult them. Let us say you are interested in Islam in Malaysia. You can immediately see which Ph.D. or M.A. student has done research work on Islam in Malaysia. You can then obtain his dissertation through inter-library loan and thus make use of material which has not been published widely but contains very valuable information.

There are other types of published sources like *monographs*, or the *festschrift*, i.e. a book in which a number of articles in honour of a scholar or important person are compiled. Some of these written sources, including series of *periodicals* may also be available in *microfilm* or *microfiche*, and the library will have a microfilm/fiche-reader for your use.

Lastly, let us consider some other sources, for example the *interview*. One can interview people by sending a letter to them and asking them certain questions. One can also meet personally and ask these questions directly.

Another very important source which many people overlook is *travelling*. During travel - if you travel in the right frame of mind, and if you are prepared for your travel and if you do not travel just to enjoy yourself on a holiday - when you have some objective, you can find out many things. It is unbelievable how much research work you can do even during a short journey. However, this has led us to the area of field research, and we shall now return to what can be done in a library.

The Library

Our next point is the location of (mostly written) information. Where do we find it?

In libraries of course. What are libraries like? This is important to know. When you go to a library like e.g. that of the School of Oriental and African Studies (SOAS) in London where they have five floors of book shelves you will not find what you want, unless you know how to use the library. Therefore in a library you need to observe a few important matters:

Firstly, there is the *card catalogue*, which you have certainly seen. Here you find information about authors, titles and the class numbers of books. A practical step for a beginner in research is to look at a library and its catalogue and to make a brief report on it, in order to familiarise himself with its system. (Some card catalogues of important libraries are also available in book-form in other libraries. Check whether the SOAS-catalogue is available in your university library before you travel to London!) Secondly, in a good library there will be a *reference section*. Here you find basic reference books, and in some way the reference collections will reflect the layout and scope of the whole library. Hence get to know it well.

A third and very important section is for *periodicals*. Go to any university library and have a look at the periodicals' section. Its huge size alone will indicate its importance.

Furthermore, it is most helpful to know the *librarian* and to have a good relationship with him. Then you can ask him any questions and he will help you to find the books you need. A good personal relationship with the librarian really counts, because the librarian is - you may be surprised - a scholar in his own right. He has spent years in the library and has accumulated a great deal of knowledge about the books. He will be glad to share this knowledge with you if he thinks you are a worthy student. Hence establish a good relationship with him.

Finally you need to know how to obtain the books, the *borrowing procedure*. One does not hide a book under one's coat and walk out; there are forms to fill in and the book will be stamped. Obtain a copy of the 'library regulations' and follow them strictly. This will give the most benefit to you and to other readers.

CREATING THE FRAMEWORK - MSC

Now we come to a very important topic: creating the framework for research. Here I want to introduce you to a formula, which I call the M-S-C code. You will not find a reference to this code elsewhere, but in my own experience I have found it very helpful and therefore I would like to share it with you.

The first step for setting the framework is to *establish priorities*. This means that once you have decided to do a research project, you should first of all take stock of all your present activities, everything that you do. Take a sheet of paper and write down a list: I sleep, I eat, I go to the shop to buy food, I visit my friends and have tea with them - all these things you already do. Write them down and do not leave out anything, because the day has only 24 hours, and whatever you do will have to fit into these 24 hours. That is why you must know what you are already doing, before you add a time-consuming research project to it.

The second step is to *evaluate* what you do. This is an application of the Q principle - asking questions. For each activity ask: why do I do this?

why do I sleep? - because I am tired (some people also sleep because they are lazy).

It may be enough to sleep six hours a day, but many people sleep eight or ten hours. Ask yourself: why do I sleep ten hours? If you do, there must be a reason for it. Perhaps you should see a doctor. Perhaps you have some health problem, since you always feel tired. Perhaps it is low blood pressure. Whatever it may be you have to look into this if it applies to you. These things do not just happen. Therefore try to find out what causes them.

Next you *eliminate* from all your activities those which from an Islamic viewpoint are not acceptable or not recommendable. If you find, according to your list of activities, that you habitually go to the cinema then you should strike that out, because from an Islamic viewpoint this is not recommendable. If you do other similar things like going to a gambling place, then you should also strike that out, because it also is not acceptable.

When you have a list of all recommendable and acceptable activities that you do, then *establish priorities*. Ask yourself six questions: The first question is when? When do I have to do it, whatever it is - today, or soon, or later, or tomorrow, or next year? It is important to know this.

For example, you want to visit a friend in Scotland. You should ask yourself: when am I going to visit him? Will this be today, or will it be next week, or will it be next month?

The second question is: how *important* is it?

The third question is: how *often* does it need to be done? Take for example 'to go to the shop to buy food'. Perhaps you go every day and buy whatever you need, but if you would only think what you need for the whole week, you could then buy it once a week. Then you need not go every day.

Fourthly, there is a very important question. If you master the art of asking and answering this question correctly, you have already done half of the task. This question is: *who else* can do that work? Do I have to do it myself or is there someone else who could do it?

For example, you are working in an Islamic organisation. You have some letters to type. At the same time you have to prepare your programme for a lecture you are to give. Can you find someone to type the letters, while you prepare your lecture, or do you have to type the letters yourself first and then prepare your lecture? This is the question to be asked. If you can find someone to do the typing this relieves you of that work and you can give your full attention to some other task.

The fifth question is: *what depends* on the activity I do? For example, you wish to win a wrestling or karate championship. You do physical training every day. How important is this? It is indeed important, because the larger objective is to win the championship, and this is the reason for your daily exercise. However, if the activity is something you decide is not essential and if there is no larger objective depending on it, then you can perhaps leave it for some time.

And lastly: is there a *better way* of doing it? With the help of these six questions you establish priorities.

The way it is described here may sound a little abstract, but if you write down what you do during the day, and if you spend 15 minutes on it, and then put the six questions to each activity. and decide and give marks: is what I do here very important, what depends on it? Can somebody else do it? - you will be surprised to discover how many things you do which are completely useless, futile and not essential in relation to your main objective.

Now let us come to the M-S-C code. After you have evaluated your activities by asking yourself these six questions, you decide that one of all the things you do, your goal, which you want to reach, *must* be done, and that is the M, it *must* be done, and it has priority.

A second kind of activity - *should* be done. This may be very important but it is less important than the first one. The third and other activities *can* be done. If you have time to spare and there is nothing else to do then you can do them.

The important thing is that in the process of planning your work you have to arrange the objectives you want to reach within this M-S-C code and then *work accordingly*. You will not do the C-category - that *can* be done - in the first place and let everything else wait. You must be clear about what to do, and the M-S-C code will help you to find out and to do it.

PROPER PLANNING - WB

Now let us deal briefly with the proper planning of things. For proper planning, you will firstly have to specify your objective: What do you want to do?

Let us say, you want to write a research paper on 'The coming of Islam to Malaysia'. Now take the next code, which we call WB.

Before you start writing your paper, you will ask - *what* has to happen *before* this? You have already specified your objective, namely, to write a research paper on 'The Coming of Islam to Malaysia'. What do you have to do *before* this? *Before* you start writing the paper? Before you write you have to know about it. Before that you have to do some research. Now break it down into the smaller steps that you have to do in research. You will want to look at the books which deal with the topic. What you have to do before this is to find the specific bibliography which gives all the references for your topics. You decide to locate this bibliography. What do you have to do before this? You have to go to the library, because that is where the bibliography is found. What do you have to do before this? You have to brush your teeth, put on your shoes and go to the library. Make yourself a plan and decide how you want to go about it. Here the important thing is *what* to do *before* it.

Let us call this procedure defining the sub-goals. A goal is an objective, and sub-goals are the parts which constitute the whole and help to achieve it. The second thing which is essential if you want to be efficient is to *allocate a time span*. For each step you decide when you will start and when you will complete it. You want to go to the library tomorrow morning at 9a.m. and you want to finish your work there by lunchtime. Unless you finish by lunchtime you cannot take the next step which you want to begin by 2p.m.

Unfortunately sometimes things do not go completely according to one's plans and the whole matter might be delayed. When planning target dates it is also very important to be flexible. If for some unforeseeable reason things do not work out the way you want them to, you must be able to adjust. If you want to go to the library and you find that the library is closed on that particular day, which you were not aware of, then you will have to adjust your plan and make it the next day.

Some people may say that planning in this manner is not the way to do Islamic work, because as Muslims we trust in Allah and everything will work out alright. There are not many *ahadīth* of the Prophet Muhammad(s) dealing with this topic but there is one which is very revealing, and I would like you to consider it:

A man said to the Prophet: 'Give me some advice', and Muhammad said: 'Judge each matter by its disposition (i.e. look at each matter by its disposition). If you see good in its outcome (i.e. if you see that its result will be good), carry on with it; but if you fear transgressing the limits set by Allah, then abstain from it'. *(A Day with the Prophet, No.114)*

The Prophet Muhammad here says very clearly: Look into the *future*, i.e. look into the result of your actions, or, in other words: do some planning. If you see the outcome will be good, carry on with it. If you see the outcome will be bad, leave it. We are employing this very principle here.

The third phase of this process is to *act*, to go *step by step*, to evaluate the work you do and to correct it and to change it whenever necessary.

Perhaps a few general hints on how to get the most out of your day would also be of benefit here. They are not only important for research work but for any kind of studies and even for your life in general whatever you want to do.

First of all look at your own routine: see how you live your day. How long is it from the first thing you do in the morning after waking up until you do something really worthwhile? This is important to know. Some people get up at six o'clock and only by ten o'clock do they start to be efficient. They take so much time to prepare their breakfast, read the newspaper, to do this and that, that four hours of their day are already wasted.

Another piece of advice is that you should avoid working at night, if possible. Sometimes being awake at night is very good. For example, I find that during Ramadan the time from *tarawih* to *fajr*-prayers is a good time for me to work. I think that Allah put more *baraka* on the nights of Ramadan. But you should not make a habit of working at night, because Allah made the daylight for your work and the night for your rest, so do not reverse the order.

Remember also that output is usually best in the morning. Get up early and try to work hard in the morning, and whatever from your M-S-C code is 'can be done' and is the least important category, leave for the afternoon.

For example, my own habit in my office is to leave the correspondence till Saturday morning. I do not generally reply to letters before Saturday unless it is a matter of greatest urgency. For me it is the C category. If I were to reply to letters daily and wrote five letters every day, it would be hours and hours wasted and I would not get to the real work which I want to do during the week. Do not bring the C category into the morning hours, but do this work in the afternoons or even at weekends.

Also try to make the morning working period quite a long one, let us say from 8a.m. to 12 o'clock. Take short breaks in between, of five minutes, one around 9a.m. and another around 10a.m. Get up from your chair, walk around and then come back to your desk and work, but do try to get a long period of uninterrupted work. That is very essential.

If someone wants to visit you, tell him in a polite way that he is welcome any time in the afternoon, but he should not come in the morning, because that is when you are working. If somebody comes unexpectedly of course you do not send him away. However, inform all whom it may concern in a polite manner about your working habits and they will understand and respect them after a time. Then you will have your time to work.

The next important principle can be learnt from the colonialists: *divide and rule.* Apply this to your daily work. Divide your daily work, then you will rule over it. If you do not divide it, it rules you and you will never get anywhere. Use the M-S-C code and ask: What *must* be done today? What *should* be done today? What *can* be done today? Then start, with what must be done, at 8 o'clock in the morning and finish it by 12 o'clock. This you do every day. That is how you get things done.

To summarise: in order to work efficiently you must first of all be clear about your objectives. Using Islamic terminology we may say that you must have the right *niyya*. That will clearly describe the purpose. Then you set the goal which you wish to achieve. Of course, you have evaluated your goal by M-S-C. After that you specify the time that you require for it. It is also important that you suppress everything that will distract you. Work in a place where you have peace of mind and where you can do your work easily.

Lastly, what happens if you fail in your research? There are four possibilities open to you:

You may *repeat* from the beginning and set right the mistakes that have occurred. For example, you may have begun some project, but you could not do your M-S-C correctly and you never really got into doing it. Start again and do the M-S-C correctly, and then you will achieve your goal.

You may also adopt a *different approach*. If you realise that the way you meant to do your project has not proved to be suitable, then try a more suitable way.

Thirdly, you may *leave* the project altogether. This can also be a good decision because at times you drag on with something which is of little value, but you do not have the courage to leave it. Then there is the fourth way: to *substitute* it by something else.

Some time ago I took a fancy to Persian poetry, but I could not really manage. Then I decided to concentrate on the language of the Qur'an instead and once I had decided that, I forgot about Persian, though I liked Persian poetry and I felt sad to leave it. But once I had decided on the language of the Qur'an, after some time and much effort, I could *al hamdu lillah* achieve something in this field which I would not have achieved if I had carried on with Persian poetry. You can learn from my experience that once you decide to leave something, there is no need to be sad about it, if you substitute something else for it which will help you to carry on.

DECIDE ABOUT THE PROJECT - OMF

So far we have looked at the framework and it is very important to observe the hints given otherwise you will not achieve anything. There is another very good formula, which I call OMF. You can use it to decide about your project. O means *objective*, and you must be clear about your objective.

For example, concerning the research paper on 'The coming of Islam to Malaysia', your objective may be to talk to a gathering of Malaysian students on this topic and therefore you need to do some research.

M stands for *motive*. Remember principle Q: asking questions:ask yourself: Why do I want to do this? There may be many motives. Sometimes the motive, because human beings are weak, may be the urge to show off to other people how much one knows. Or someone might push you into it. You do not want to do it, but someone compels you to do it, and in some way you have to respond. Or there may be the motive that you think you know something about this topic, which you can share with others. There may be many motives, but you must be clear in each case what your motive is.

Lastly, F stands for *feasibility*. Is it feasible to do it? You are to decide about the research topic. You want to do a paper on 'The Coming of Islam to Malaysia'. You do not know the Malay language. Is it then feasible for you to do that work? Feasibility is very important. The motive is your inner urge, the reason you wish to do it. The objective establishes what you wish to achieve with it. Feasibility shows whether or not you can do it.

There are some factors which help to decide about that. Ask for example: is it easy to reach all resource material, or is it very difficult? You may want to do some study on the Muhammadiya in Indonesia or a similar group. Is this feasible for you? Have you ever met somebody from the Muhammadiya? Is there at least any book in your library on Muhammadiya, so that you can start this project? These are some of the questions you have to ask, and sometimes you have to have the courage to say: No, it is not feasible, I shall leave it. I shall do it some other time, when it is feasible and for now I shall concentrate on something which is within my reach.

INPUT

Now we come to the input. Once you have decided about the research project you will begin to put effort into it.

Reading is the most important way of input. Another way is to *listen*, to what we hear in lectures, talks, discussions, etc.

There is a difference between reading that just recognises words and between study, i.e. to observe what the words mean. For example, you may not be very good at mathematics and physics, but you can read a dozen books on physics in one week if you are not required to make sense out of what you read. For research work you have to make sure that what you read you also *understand*.

In the beginning be quite sure that you have the proper pre-information about the book. What are the book's issues? Who is the author? What else did he write? What about the preface, what does it explain? From the preface you may already conclude certain things.

Look at the *introduction*, go through the list of *contents* and familiarise yourself with the book. Only after you have done that, decide whether you really need to read the book or not. Far better to spend a few minutes gathering this sort of pre-information, than taking the book home and wasting a lot of time on it.

Once you begin reading the book, *avoid bias* from the first to last page. It may be unfamiliar to some of you, but I would say: do not have any bias, even when you read an orientalist's book on Islam. First of all, hear what the author has to say. Analyse it later on, but first let him speak. This is the better style and right behaviour (adab) to let people say what they have to say and not to interrupt them after the second sentence: No, this is rubbish and we shall throw it away. If you are interested in the topic, hear what the writer has to say and after that analyse it.

Next *form your own opinion*. You may be very aggressive in your language - while you talk to yourself. When you talk to people you should be polite, but while you talk to yourself aggressiveness will help you to clarify things in your mind.

Apply the principle Q - ask questions concerning what the author has written. Question him and say: You cannot say this; that chapter and that paragraph reveal your mistakes. How can you come to this conclusion?, etc.

Ask him: Are you properly qualified to undertake this type of research? Question the author and form your own opinion about whatever he has written. When you complete a chapter or a section of the book, stop for a while and recall in your mind what he has said. Usually at the end of a chapter there is some blank space, half a page or so. Note down, if it is your own book, in a few words, *in pencil,* the importance of this chapter. If it is a book from a library or a friend, do not mark the book because other people may be very annoyed about this. Write your notes on a small piece of paper. When, after two years, you read a certain book again, you may be very disappointed that your two-year-old poor knowledge has been inscribed permanently. You may now erase your pencilled notes and write something else in their place.

My most complicated formula is the formula $SQR^3 + E$. It is very important for the proper reading of books:

S stands for 'make a *survey* of the book', i.e. look at the author, the list of contents, the index, the bibliography. Make a general survey of the book.

Secondly, Q of course stands for *question.* While you read, question whatever the author says. If he says that Islam came to Malaysia because the British government was so generous as to allow it in, question that, and if you read that Islam came to Malaysia because people from Sumatra migrated to Malacca, question that, and if someone writes that Islam came to Malaysia because merchants came from India to the North of Kedah, question that as well. First you question everything that is written there and then you formulate your own opinion. Do not accept anything as valid until you are reasonably sure it is correct.

The first of the three R's is to *read,* and you have already read a few things about it, namely how to read and to pause after each chapter, then to think about what you have read, and to formulate your own opinion. The second R stands for *recall,* i.e. recall the important passages by summarising them. In pencil write a few notes at the end of each chapter. This is the summary and recall. The third R means *revise.* If the book is important for you, then revise what you have read, in your mind, on the same day. Do the mental exercise of going through it: that's what he wrote in this chapter, this is his opinion and my opinion is such and such.

Finally, E stands for *evaluate*. After you have gone through all these stages then you evaluate the book as a whole and you conclude: the book is useful for your research, or only some parts of it are useful and which are those parts, etc.

There are many more hints one can give: how to read faster, etc., but we shall not go into these details here. However, be sure of one thing: whenever you read, have a *pencil* at hand. Read the book and make notes as you progress. If it is a library book make notes on a piece of paper. In any case *take notes*.

Whenever there is a definition in the chapter somewhere, I usually write *def.* in the margin. You can use whatever abbreviations you like, but do develop some kind of system. When I find something questionable I make a ? and when I find something important I mark it ! When I want to indicate the key word in a sentence I mark an arrow in the margin and circle the key word. You should develop such symbols for yourself, and you should use them in order to become faster in your reading and revising. Reading speed is very important to cover the most ground.

While doing all this reading and taking notes you may find your mind wandering. When you realise that you are thinking about something else, about going home, wanting to see your parents, asking why are you sitting here, when would you be with your friends? etc., then try to tell yourself: I shall work through this, another 15 minutes more and then I will be finished. You will then concentrate again.

The other thing is that after reading or listening to something you let it work in your mind and try next week to remember the things read or said. Let them work in your mind. You will be surprised how many new ideas you yourself will generate, not things which you have read or someone has told you, but ideas coming from your own mind, from your own experience. Let, whatever you put in, work in your mind and realise that it is *you* who is thinking and then make use of the ideas that you are generating.

Secondly, let us look at *lectures*. How does one really learn from a lecture and how does one get information from it?

First of all, not every lecture that you attend will be useful to you. Whenever you intend to go to a lecture, first use principle Q and ask: why is it important for me to go there?

Often people go to lectures simply because they feel that if they do not show their faces someone else might be disappointed. However, if we are dedicated to our Islamic work, we do not have time to waste for things that are not essential. This should not mean that from now on you do not go to lectures any more. You will still go to lectures, but beforehand you will decide carefully: is it worthwhile going or not? Sometimes you may only realise during the early stages of a lecture whether you will benefit from it or not. You may find lecturers who give a clear outline at the beginning of the lecture, and you can see whether it is going to be of interest to you or not. If it is not of interest to you, then do have the courage to leave the hall because there are other things for you to do which are more important, and if it is of interest to you then stay and listen, even if the lecture is in the end longer than anticipated. When a lecturer does not tell you at the beginning what he is going to say, then in my view he is not a very good lecturer and he perhaps has not decided yet what he is going to say. He will just make up his mind while talking, and whatever comes into his mind, he will say to you. Few people are indeed brilliant, but some do have considerable experience. They can speak without preparation on many a topic you might give them. They may speak even on the rotation of the moon, and you could still benefit from them. But such people are very rare, and usually when someone cannot tell you at the beginning what he intends to say then it may be better to leave and let him talk to other people.

You should also prefer, when you have a choice, lectures which allow you to participate, because *learning is through participation.* You may for example, have the choice between a lecturer in the university who will through the whole term just lecture and lecture and lecture and another lecturer who will invite you to take up certain topics and to present them in the classroom, who will encourage you to do your own research work, and to challenge other people's views. You should choose the second one, because that is how you will really learn and become trained.

Lastly, do not note down every word that is being said, but *note* down *the key words* and the structure of the lecture. In fact when somebody tells you at the beginning what he is going to talk about, you will know and note the structure first of all and then, while you listen, you can just fill in the gaps and such issues which are important to you. Therefore it is essential for a good lecture to be preceded by the outline and to be summarised at the end. The latter is the time for you to go through your notes and to see whether you have everything complete, and if you do not have, then there should be at question time the opportunity to ask questions about the *lecture*, not about something else in your mind which you perhaps have wanted to ask for a long time. You will notice this type of question being asked by many audiences, but if you note down the outline of the talk and then, while the lecturer summarises, go through it and see whether you have got everything correct, you will concentrate on whatever you missed, and in this way you will benefit more from lectures.

Lastly, there is one more method of in-put, which is in fact a kind of mixed lecture, and you can also benefit from it: T.V. and radio.

Use the same techniques as for the lecture. For example, take the many programmes which reported on the riots in the inner cities of this country. There were some useful discussions in the media on this and while watching one could take a few notes: who was speaking? Who was saying what? At the end of the programme, we could go through the notes and then unless we needed them for something special, they could be thrown away. But we participated in some way in this T.V. debate, we formulated our own views and we clarified them in our mind. With this technique you do not simply watch T.V., but really benefit from it. Of course there are many programmes on T.V. which we do not even want to watch, but some broadcasts are also helpful and informative.

Keeping notes

You may have collected a number of sources containing information for your topic of research, be it in the form of books, articles, lecture notes, etc. It is most important that you keep them in an orderly fashion, otherwise you will soon be lost in the amount of paper gathered.

There are two common ways of keeping notes. Either use cards (small or large, depending on the type of work you do, or perhaps both), or use a notebook.

Small cards are very suitable for keeping references of books, while larger cards can be used for excerpts and quotations. A notebook can be used in a similar fashion. However make sure that you do not have more than one item/idea/quote on a page, since at a later stage you may perhaps take out the pages from the notebook to arrange them in alphabetical (or some other) order.

Always leave space at the top or in the margin for a key-word, which will help you to distinguish, at a glance, one card (or page) from another, and never omit the complete reference, which should be at the bottom of the page. Otherwise you may have great difficulty retracing your source, whenever you need to check or amend it: author, title, year of publication, page number. Use boxes with guide-cards (alphabetical or key-word index) to store your material. The cheapest form of box comes from shoe shops. They are well suited for taking notes of A-5 size.

Do not write on the back of a card or page, unless it is the continuation of matter noted down on the front. If you use both sides of the cards for different items, you will very soon become confused and not know what you have done, when you did it and where you keep it.

You might think that this is a waste of paper and cards, but this is not so. You can always strike out the material on cards, after you have completed your project and have no further use for the references, and then use the blank reverse of the same cards for your next project.

It is also very helpful to keep a small notebook (or some cards) for pending matters, i.e. books or articles you wish to consult during your next visit to the library, verification of some figures and data you came across etc. Strike out each item, after you have dealt with it and keep the result on fresh cards (pages), but *not* in that notebook:.

Also, do not be deceived by the extremely easy use of the photocopying machine. Make photocopies only of such material that will not be accessible to you otherwise (i.e. where you cannot borrow the book, journal or document to look at in detail in the library or your own place of study), but do not think that by merely copying pages you have 'made notes'. In fact you will have to look at the copies again and spend as much time and effort to read, grasp, excerpt, etc. as you did when you consulted the original piece.

When making notes, do not simply copy what you have before you unless it is a direct quotation that you need - this could be done by the photocopying machine much faster and with less risk of error. Note only what you require from the paragraph or chapter in question. The author's aim in writing has in most cases been different from your own in researching. Re-phrase and shorten, whenever possible. Use abbreviations where suitable (for often occurring names of persons, cities, etc.) but do not get confused. Use a clear and simple system.

Whenever you note - on the same piece of paper - some ideas of your own, distinguish them clearly (by, e.g. putting them in square brackets [   ] and include your initials.

OUTPUT

When you begin to write you should first of all make a very rough *outline* of what you intend to do. Do not write everything on a single sheet of paper but use separate sheets for each chapter or each part and note down what belongs to it. Then prepare a rough list of contents by arranging your sheets of paper in their proper order. Often things come to one's mind not in the proper order, and by noting them on loose leaves or sheets you can easily arrange them. If you look at your material and realise that a certain part is out of place and should be moved to another place, then you simply move it to that place, etc. This technique will save you striking out, throwing away, using a new sheet, writing a few words, still no good, throwing away again, etc. It is best to write on small sheets first. Then make more detailed notes of the important issues, but do not go into too much detail because that will be done in the final stage.

WRITING

Be aware of the fact that your first piece of writing on a subject will in almost all cases be a 'draft' version. Let a few days (or even weeks) elapse and then go over it again. Clarify what you now see as inadequately explained or expressed. Tighten the language and aim for a more precise vocabulary. Prune out all side issues and concentrate on the main questions (if some important side issue needs to be briefly referred to, transfer it to a footnote, or an appendix). This will make matters clearer to yourself and your straightforward and clear style will also attract the reader.

A FORMULA FOR WRITING: LBC(S)

When you write something use a very simple formula which we will call LBC(S).

L means *lead*, which is borrowed from the journalist's jargon. You may also use the word introduction. It leads the reader into the topic. The second section in a piece of writing is the *body:* B. The third section is the *conclusion:* C; and what has been put in brackets(S), is the *summary*, which may not always be necessary.

You will find that 99% of all pieces of writing have this kind of structure and consist of *lead, body, conclusion* and *summary:* LBC (S).

Let us take an example: we shall just make up a small piece of information. In it the L will be its key sentence informing the reader what it is all about. The body will be the elaboration, and the conclusion will be the last part which relates to the first. In this way we wrap the whole thing up. Here is the example (hopefully of use not only to researchers but to some amateur cooks too!).

The lead: 'A quick method of making chappatis'.

Now the body: 'If you are pressed for time and your guests are waiting, you should make two chappatis at one time. Put some oil on top of the first one and place the second one on top of it and fry them together'. That was B, the elaboration and how to do it.

Now comes C, the conclusion: 'This way your guests will not have to wait too long'.

This is in agreement with the first statement, namely that it is a quick method of making chappatis.

With these four sentences you have a good model. You may choose your topic freely. You may want to write a small article for a journal or a newsletter. Perhaps something happened in your weekly meeting that you want to share with other people, or any other small piece of writing. It is always helpful to use this pattern:

Start with the lead,

prepare the body,

end with the conclusion.

There are of course many other forms of writing. Let us take 'Letters to the Editor'. They are written in response to some article, and have the same pattern - lead, body, conclusion, and if it does not have these, then the editor would be wise to reject it because it will be confusing. If the person who writes such a letter cannot explain what he wants to in a few words and he needs more space then there would be no room for his view in the journal or newspaper.

When you write a *biographical note* about someone, for example about one of the Companions of the Prophet Muhammad (s), you would use the same pattern. Use the lead to introduce him, i.e. giving his name, when he was born, etc. Then comes the body, where you tell whatever you know about him and finally comes the conclusion which sums up his major contributions for Islam.

You may also write a *commentary*. Select an issue which is important. Of course you first do your research so that you have your facts well organised, before you begin writing. For example, a topic which I believe to be very important but which I have never found anyone writing about, is that of young Muslim students, and of female Muslim students in particular, who are here in this country without father, brother or husband. There are many such students here, and someone should write a commentary on this issue. Of course he could use the same formula. Firstly he could give the facts, then explain the pros and cons and then evaluate. In the conclusion he could try to suggest some solution. He should not expect that because of his writing everything will change immediately and the whole world will be different from today. But he will make some people aware of the problems while explaining the situation. You may also write *news items*. The same formula applies except that there is no need for a conclusion. News items simply have L, which tells the reader what it is all about, followed by B, which is arranged in declining order. The last sentence of the news item is usually the least important whereas the first one is most important.

You may also write *book reviews*. To write such reviews is very valuable because first you must read the book thoroughly and this helps you to understand the book. The published review helps other people to know about the book. The lead will be about the book and its author, and the body will discuss: what does the author want to achieve with his book? and did he succeed or not? You will summarise the contents. Then you will touch upon the controversial issues and its valid and weak arguments. Finally, you will recommend the book or not.

You write an *article* by applying the same formula, the LBC(S); you recall S means summary, i.e. at the end of the conclusion you summarise the main ideas of the article. With the L you draw the reader's attention to what you want to say. Then you present your case in the B and then if you have some advice or a suggestion you give it and then you conclude. Basically it is always the same principle.

Finally, after you have done research work you are also in a position to organise a *class* or organise a *course* and to share with other people in this field what you have achieved. But this is another area altogether, which we shall not pursue here.

Conclusion

Let us summarise briefly the few formulas which I have introduced to you:

The first was the MSC code, which concerned things which *must* be done, which *should* be done, which *can* be done. It helps you to get your *priorities* right and also to plan your time properly.

The *time planning* itself is done with the WB - what before this. When you plan your research you will ask this question.

For input, the important things concerning the *reading* were in the SQR(3) + E, namely survey, question, read, recall, which means to remember what you read, and to make a note of it, revise (that is to look at it again if you want to keep it in your mind) and finally E, to evaluate it.

As far as the *output* is concerned, we used LBC(S) the lead (the introduction), the body, the conclusion and the summary.

Lastly, I wish to emphasise OMF, objective, motive, feasibility. When you *decide* about a research project, first establish the objective (what), and then clarify the motive (why), and if after critical evaluation you find that the motive was not right according to Islamic values then leave it and do not do it. There are three issues concerning feasibility and we shall discuss one of them in more detail when we talk about Islamic research. This is the question whether from an Islamic viewpoint something is useful or important and this question will determine in our Muslim view the feasibility though perhaps not in the view of a non-Muslim researcher. The second issue concerns qualification, i.e. whether you are capable of tackling the subject you have selected. Thirdly there is need to have the resource material available. Last but not least you have to ask: do I have time for it? That question will again be answered by MSC. These are the basic principles for assessing feasibility.

SECTION II

ISLAMIC PRINCIPLES FOR RESEARCH WORK

Now let us look at the Islamic criteria for research work. You will remember that the first principle in research is Q, i.e. asking questions. For Islamic research we re-define it as Q(2), i.e. asking *questions* about the *Qur'an*, because the Qur'an is the basis of all our Islamic knowledge, our Islamic behaviour and our Islamic actions. Indeed the second important condition for Islamic research is that it must somehow be related to action. Knowledge separated from its proper application is useless in the Islamic perspective. This is one of the basic differences between Islam and other philosophies or sciences. Generally people hold that simply to acquire knowledge is already of some value but as Muslims we disagree. Knowledge properly applied is the only knowledge we cherish.

To take guidance from the Qur'an, and to ask questions about the Qur'an with the objective of applying whatever we learn in this manner requires understanding the message of the Qur'an, and for this there are two important points we have to bear in mind.

Firstly: to study the Qur'an,

secondly: to learn the language of the Qur'an.

I shall dwell on these a little for both topics are very important. The importance of the Arabic language has been emphasised many times. I myself prefer to distinguish between the 'Arabic' language and the *Language of the Qur'an*. Some may think that this is not proper but it is my conviction that the language of the Qur'an differs from the language of the Arabs as we have it today. We usually employ the term 'Arabic language' as a short description of what we want to say, but in fact we are concerned with the language of the Qur'an. That is the language we have to learn.

The order to study the Qur'an and learn the language I give with clear intention. Study of the Qur'an comes first and secondly to learn the language of the Qur'an, because it is clear, both due to theoretical insight as well as through experience that if you were to delay study of the Qur'an until you had mastered its language you would waste a long time before applying knowledge from the Qur'an. Therefore study the Qur'an even though you do not yet know the language. In this case use translation and interpretation, and keep before you its limitations, but do not delay study of the Qur'an until you have mastered its language.

There are some very important points about how to study the Qur'an, not only for the sake of Islamic research work but for your way of life as a whole. Islamic research work as part of a Muslim's life and actions is based on a proper understanding of the Qur'an, and that is why you need to understand the Qur'an properly. Here are a few suggestions for anyone, whether he knows the language or not, whether he uses a translation or the original book.

First of all remember that like any other effort of a Muslim you study the Qur'an and aim to understand it for the sake of Allah, and not for any other purpose. Your *niya* must be clear.

Here are a few practical suggestions: get an exercise book, write on it: 'Study of the Qur'an', and do not write anything else in this book except what concerns your study of the Qur'an. If you follow this suggestion you will soon realise that after a short time, even after a few weeks, this exercise book will be one of the most valuable reference and research materials that you may ever have, because it will contain notes on the basic themes of the Qur'anic message together with *your* own reactions to them and *your* understanding of them. Thirdly I suggest you read a short article by Khurram Murad entitled: 'The Way to the Qur'an'. (1) While reading it you should make notes for a brief outline of it, using key words so that you will become deeply familiar with its main ideas.

Thus prepared you do one short study on the Qur'an per week. Decide yourself what your study unit will be, for example one *ruku'* would be an easy unit per week, or, if you can do more than this, then do so, whatever you can really master. Even if you decide to study only ten *ayas* per week that is a good procedure. If you can do your study in a study circle this will be of great advantage because Muslims ought to study the Qur'an together. Otherwise do it by yourself. Initially you should not spend too much time on it, perhaps not more than 15 or 20 minutes. First read the passage in the language that is best known to you, be it Malay, Urdu, English, Hausa, Arabic or whatever else. Never omit though to read the Arabic text along with it.

---

1.   This article is included in Ali, A.Y., *The Holy Qur'ān: Text, Translation, Commentary*. The Islamic Foundation, Leicester, 1978. It will soon be available (inshallah) in an expanded version as a separately printed book.

First read it in your mother tongue and then the Arabic text. Do not look at the footnotes and explanations until you have thought out for yourself the meaning of the passage. Try not to be influenced by the opinions of translators or writers, but instead listen first to the message of the Qur'an speaking to you. Ask yourself: what does this verse mean for *me?*. That is what is really important.

Let us take a simple example. You will come across many verses of the Qur'an mentioning the *munafiqun* (hypocrites). The footnotes will explain to you that these *munafiqun* were people who lived at the time of Prophet Muhammad. In fact they were one of several groups namely the *muhajirun*, the *ansar*, the *munafiqun*, the *ahl al-kitab*, the *kafirun*, the *mushriks*, etc. The *munafiqun* were from Madina and they behaved in a certain way. You might erroneously think that the question of *munafiqun* is a matter of the past, as explained in the footnotes. (2)

It is very important to realise that each verse of the Qur'an has a meaning for us, and hence when we speak about *munafiqun* we have to ask ourselves: does that refer to me?

Yes, the Qur'an may here speak about you and if it speaks about you then you have to change, you have to change yourself so that you do not keep any of the traits of character of the *munafiqun*. However, if you read the footnotes first and then decide that this issue is a matter of the past alone and does not exist today you will never come to ask this question about yourself. That is why it is important to listen to the Qur'an first, and not be guided exclusively by the interpretations of other people. Later on you will also read what they have to say but initially you must listen only to the Qur'an. Next think of a simple phrase or statement that will summarise the paragraph you have studied. We might say that you make a *headline* for it. This phrase or headline you note in your excercise book. For example, you enter the reference Sura 2: 27-35 and then add the headline, which explains the contents of these verses. In the next line you note down the important point or points which you think are expressed here. For this you have to look at the passage with some care and not just over-read it. Think and ask: what does it mean, what is the important point here? Then note it down.

---

2. See also my article, 'The Signs of the Munafiq', in: *The Muslim* (London), 16 (1), 1980, 12-13.

If there is any open *question*, note it down. Never be afraid to admit that there are some open questions. Remember principle Q. The most knowledgeable person is the one who asks questions, not the person who avoids all questions. If the question can be answered in your study circle, then note down the reply as well. If not, leave it open and when you come to another place in the Qur'an where you find the answer to this question, note it down, or, if you do not come across the answer ask someone who has your confidence, and of whom you know has insight into the Qur'an, and he may try to help you. In this manner it is easy to fill such gaps, and there is no need to be shy about asking questions. This is really important, because asking questions is, as I told you, the basic principle of research.

You should also pay attention to the correct recitation of the Qur'an, though not necessarily in the study circle. You can do that at home or at some other time. You can also learn from a cassette. Use the study circle to grasp the *meaning* of the Qur'an. As a prerequisite for deeper Islamic research you must know the Qur'an and its message and for this you also need to have some knowledge of the language of the Qur'an.(3) However, I cannot go into details here.

Next are a few points on research and Islam. Firstly, the question may arise: should Muslims do research on Islam? Well I think that we should. Some people may disagree with this but their opinion is not valid. Sura 9: 122 clearly advises the Muslims that not all of them should go to Jihad but that some of them should stay behind and get more insight into Islam in order that they can help other people to understand Islam. This shows that even during a time of Jihad when the physical struggle for survival of Islam takes place, the Qur'an suggests that some Muslims should devote their time to a better understanding of Islam. From this verse it is clear that what we call research in Islam, i.e. efforts for a better understanding of Islam, for some Muslims is a duty as valuable and as important as physical Jihad.

---

3.   There is not really any suitable book available for this purpose, although many books on 'Arabic language' exist. A course entitled 'Learn the Language of the Qur'an' using an entirely new approach and designed specifically for Muslims whose mother tongue is not Arabic and who wish to learn the language to understand the Qur'an, has been prepared and is in its first experimental teaching. It will, inshallah, be published soon.

Two other questions we should be aware of are: who is the Islamic worker and what is research generally? Again this is not the place to go into detail, but we may define the Islamic worker as a person who is fully dedicated to give in the most suitable way whatever ability and talent he has for the sake of establishing Islam. The concept of research has been covered in the previous section.

Next let us distinguish between research *in Islam*, which can also be called Islamic studies, and what might be called research *for Islamic work*. While research in Islam (Islamic studies) will generally be confined to specific themes and areas of study, research for Islamic work cannot be restricted to any area because of Islam's nature as an all comprehensive way of life. Any aspect of our life is concerned with Islam and therefore any aspect of our life can and must be followed up by research for Islamic work.

Of course in the field of society where Islam should be applied, there will be the greatest need for research for Islamic work. You may ask: why not also in physics, biochemistry or similar fields? Because in these fields of creation the law of Allah is already fully applied - what we call the laws of Allah, and man is simply discovering them. In society on the other hand, the law of Allah, although applied in one way (because nothing happens in this world without the will of Allah) is today not specifically applied in human society at large. That is why we have to concentrate on putting into practice in society the revealed will of Allah and hence there is great need for research for Islamic work.

Let us look at a few examples. What kind of research could you do for Islamic work? For example, in the field of Da'wa we need to distinguish *Tawḥīd* from *Shirk*. We need to discover the contemporary forms of *Shirk*. For this purpose we have to research into people's motivations, into ideologies, into people's thinking and world-views. In this way we can grasp the contemporary forms of *Shirk* and then put them into contrast with Tawhid in order to invite people to Islam, which is the message flowing from Tawhid.

Another example may be taken from the field of economics. Here we have to research into the question of how to replace the prevalent system of economics which is based on *Ribā*, because Riba is against the will of Allah. However, by stating simply or in an elaborate way that it is against the will of Allah and by wishing it would be changed will not make it disappear. This replacement needs to be done by Muslims and in order to do it we have to know how it can be done. We have to research into it, to find the methods to change it.

Another example may be taken from the field of biochemistry. I said earlier that such an area might be less important, but it has its importance too. We need to find substitutes for alcohol which is used in most medicines today, because even though in some schools of law alcohol is perhaps allowed for medical purposes we would like to, if we can, avoid it altogether. The bio-chemist can find substitutes. Or take the case of cheese production; cannot a Muslim scientist find substitutes for renin and rennet which are used in cheese production? We should eat cheese because actually it is a very healthy food, but often we do not do so because we fear it is produced in an unclean way. Hence if our Muslim scientists can do research and find substitutes this is also research for the sake of Islam and very valuable indeed.

However, let us go back to the first example. In the field of Da'wa research has at least two dimensions: one of which concerns us Muslims. If we can clarify the issues we shall bring more commitment to the Muslim worker, to the individual involved, to ourselves. When we clarify certain issues through research, our own conviction of the correct Islamic view on certain issues will grow and be reassured. We do not simply *believe* that Islam is the right way, we *know* it is, on the basis of our own research, and this makes our conviction grow. The other aspect is that we can invite and convince other people. When we put our case in a way which is reasonable and acceptable to people who can use their own judgement then there is certainly more room for convincing them and bringing them nearer to Islam.

The starting point of all research for Islamic work is to relate the Islamic way of life to the *status quo*, i.e. the situation of today. We have to look at two things: how things are now, and what Islam wants.

Of course the objective is to bring about change from the *status quo* to the application of Islamic norms and values. We do not do that as mere intellectual play. We apply our knowledge to bring about that change. I recommend strongly that we first cover this area concerning the relationship between the *status quo* and Islamic values in research before we tackle other questions, both in-dividually and as a community. For example, at the North and South Poles there is no real day and night at certain times of the year. How do we pray there, and how do we fast? These are quite interesting questions and to some extent important too but they do not have first priority. First priority must be given to questions which are concerned with the present situation in society, with Islamic values and with the change of society towards the application of Islamic values. Here I come back to the MSC-code: what must be done; is this kind of research about the present situation, Islamic values and change.

Another side issue is also important: through research we must free Islamic knowledge from certain changes which have crept into it. We must be able to distinguish between the message of the Qur'an and Sunna and the interpretation which it has obtained throughout history. This also we can achieve through research in Islam. In particular, we should do research on the Qur'an and Sunna, in order that we understand the message properly. We need to know more especially about those Ahadith which are concerned with *tafsīr*, in order to get a clear picture of the original meaning of the message of the Qur'an. We want to do away with the Christian and Jewish interpretations and the Greek philosophy and all that people are selling to us today as 'Islamic knowledge'. For example, a well-known Malaysian scholar wrote a book on Islamic education, but the book is full of Greek philosophy, and he is trying to explain this as Islamic education. There is hardly any reference to the Qur'an and Sunna in the whole discussion on education. This is happening today, in our society, not a thousand years ago, when Greek thinking and philosophy was studied by Muslims.

Through research again we may expose that mysticism, called Sufism, which many people do not realise, destroys Islam and the Islamic movement. Many of those who today propagate *Tassawuf* have never spoken or acted for the people in the Muslim societies who are suppressed. They speak only about the 'mystic dimensions'. They do not speak about the injustice that is happening in front of our eyes nor do they act against it. Well-known authors write numerous books about Sufism, *Tassawuf* and perennial philosophy, and a whole group of very intelligent and clever people try to distract young Muslims from the real issues and try to lead them into the 'mystic approach', which has nothing to do with Islamic work. There are many young people who have been deceived in this way.

I said at the beginning that Islamic research is for all fields of knowledge and all fields of application because Islam is for the whole world. Our Islamic research must therefore not be restricted to any particular country. If we want to change society today, it must be in a world-wide dimension. What Islam offers to Malaysia it can also offer to the U.K., to Egypt, to Nigeria, to any other part of the world. That is the Islamic approach. Only when we discuss some minor issues, from the C-category might we restrict ourselves to a particular country but while we do research for Islamic work we talk about basic issues and these pertain to the whole world. The problems of modern society for example such as alcoholism, abortion, breakdown of the family, etc., are universal. Look at the anti-Islamic philosophies and the anti-Islamic movements. We have to research into them. To know our opponents is the only way to defeat them. We also have to expose universal secularism, but especially we have to make up, through our research work, for 'disorientation through the educational system', because all of us go through educational systems which disorientate us from the Islamic view and the Islamic way of life. We have to make up for this through research, to increase our knowledge about the Islamic way of life.

Lastly I want to touch briefly upon the prerequisites for you as an Islamic research worker. You must have a true *taqwā*, and you must have the right relationship with your Creator. Secondly you need the proper knowledge and competence in your field of study. It is not sufficient to have only the will to do some research work. If you cannot do it, if you are not able to do it, then you are better to stay away from it. You must have a good knowledge of Islam, and if it is serious research you must know the language of the Qur'an. You must be independent in your thinking, and apply what I have called the Q factor: you must be able to ask the right questions.

You must also be free of vested interests. This means to be able to ask the right questions in any situation and under any circumstances. Today we find in the Muslim world that our scholars in research, for example in political or social sciences, avoid certain basic questions because the people who are in power would feel uncomfortable. if these questions were to be asked. You have to ask: why is your economy still based on *Ribā?* There is talk about Islamisation in some Muslim countries, but they do not ask about the economy. If you do *Islamic* research you cannot do that, you cannot exclude certain issues, you have to ask questions in all fields.

And lastly, you must practise what you preach. This is very important. I said there is no use doing Islamic research unless we apply it. This means that whatever we preach we must practise. There should be no distinction between our words and our actions, they must be the same. This may be different for other research work, but for the Islamic worker it has to be like this.

As far as our methods are concerned we hold that firstly all the principles from the Qur'an and Sunna have priority. Later sources, like the writings of Muslim scholars, the *fuqaha* and whoever else, are very important but of secondary importance. First come the Qur'an and Sunna, and then come the later scholars.

Thirdly, reason must be given its proper place. Reason can even be ranked second and the opinion of the earlier scholars third. We are not obliged to follow the opinions of Muslim scholars only because they belong to earlier generations. If reason shows that their application is not useful for us, we can do without them, but as far as the Qur'an and Sunna are concerned we have to observe their guidance under all circumstances.

Fourthly, we have to realise that our research may not bring the results that we hope for. If we were non-Muslim research workers we might close the chapter and walk away. But as a Muslim we have to communicate whatever results we find. We cannot avoid the consequences of our research even if it is inconvenient for us. A very simple example is that perhaps 10 or 15 years ago few people were concerned about eating cheese and most people used to eat it without question. When someone made research into cheese production and he found that a substance is used which is not *halāl* he had two choices: he could keep quiet, leaving things as they were or communicate his findings. As a Muslim he was obliged to communicate his findings even if it was inconvenient.

Let us take another example. You are from Malaysia and do research about Islam in Malaysia. You anticipate, while doing this study that you will discover that the colonial powers are the cause for the historical decline of Islam in Malaysia. But during your research you may well discover that the real cause for the decline of Islam in Malaysia was the disease in the leadership of the Muslims during the time of the colonialists. Your research has given you facts which you do not like to admit. Now your dilemma may be: they were Malays, you are Malay. It is easy to blame the white man for all the problems. Furthermore, we Muslims should not cause friction amongst ourselves...

But as a Muslim, if you find that the cause lies in your own ranks you will have to admit that and you will have to try to rectify it.

To conclude let us look at a quotation from Ibn Khaldun, one of the well-known scholars, who lived in the fourteenth century. He wrote an important book, the *Muqqadima* in which he discussed a great variety of topics, one among them being education. My comments to his words are in brackets. He wrote:

'The natural means for the perception of truth is...man's natural ability to think.' (This means: because you can think you can discover the truth. This is the natural way.)

'When it is free from all misgivings and when the thinker entrusts himself to the mercy of God.' (So you relate your thinking to Allah, then you can discover the truth, that is the natural way.)

'Logic merely describes the process of thinking and mostly parallels it. Take that into consideration and ask for God's mercy when you have difficulty in understanding problems.' (So realise that by logic you do not achieve the results because logic only describes the process, it does not bring the result, and when you have difficulty in understanding, then call to Allah, for He is the one who can give you the knowledge.)

'Then (when you ask for Allah's mercy) the divine light will shine upon you and give you the right inspiration. God guides in His mercy. Knowledge comes only from God.' (4)

---

4.   *Muqqadima* III, 298.

SECTION III

PRACTICAL ASSIGNMENTS AND EXERCISES

The following section is as important for you as the two previous ones. Do not put this book aside until you have completed all the assignments given here. You do not have to do them all in one day, but try to accomplish them without too much delay.

Why assignments? You know that learning comes largely through *doing* things. You have to *apply* what you have learnt so far. Through practise you will discover shortcomings and mistakes, you will then have many opportunities for improvement. For me, conducting this course was an excellent exercise to improve my own performance in many areas from research, planning and preparation to teaching, evaluation, human relations and *'ibāda*.

Assignment No. 1

Go to your local library (university or college library) and get to know

- the card-catalogue (authors and subjects)
- the classification system
- the periodical section
- the reference section
- the lending procedures
- the librarian to assist you

Lastly, locate and borrow a book on research work and browse through it to revise what you have learnt so far.

Assignment No. 2

Visit the library section of your local Muslim organisation (mosque) and make yourself familiar with it. Prepare a brief note on its advantages and shortcomings.

Later, on an appropriate occasion you may also share this with the person responsible for that library section.

Exercise No.1 : Prepare a reading list on the topic 'Women in Islam'.

Assignment No. 3

Select five useful books for a student, who wishes to learn more about 'Marriage and Divorce' in Islam.

Exercise No.2 : Analyse the 'Preface' to A. Guillaume's book *The Traditions of Islam.* (5)(Oxford; and reprints).

Exercise No.3 : Read and mark (with pencil) the Introduction by G. Margoliouth to Rodwell's translation (5) of the Qur'an.

Exercise No.4 : Analyse any interview-article published in the magazine *Impact International, Muslim Viewpoints on Current Affairs* (London) bearing in mind the guidelines given in Section I.

Assignment No. 4

Prepare a brief description of the book *Mishkat al-Masabih*, translated by James Robson (Ashraf, Lahore).

Assignment No. 5

Write a short review on the booklet *Growing up in Islam*, by T.B. Irving. (Leicester)

Assignment No. 6

Read the following notes on the Islamic Foundation and assume that you have obtained this information during a visit you have paid there.

Write a 150-words news item on 'your' visit to the Islamic Foundation. Add your own questions, which have not been dealt with in this note.

Assignment No. 7

Prepare a topical study on *du'a*, e.g. 'The concept of "calling unto God" in Islam'. Outline both collection of material (from which sources?) and arrangement of material (list of contents).

---

5.   You will find this book in most bigger libraries. If not available, order it through inter-library loan. Do not buy it.

British 'think tank' plays unique role

The Islamic Foundation in Leicester is an independent research unit with a strong interest in spreading Islam through education.

SITUATED IN AN elegant 18th century mansion near the university in the British Midlands town of Leicester is a unique Muslim institution. But its uniqueness does not please its director, Mr Khurram Murad: "There is so much to be done that we wish there were hundreds of similar places," he says.

First conceived in 1973 by a group of mainly Pakistani, Indian and Bangladeshi Muslims led by the well-known Islamic economist Professor Khursid Ahmad, the Islamic Foundation moved into its present headquarters in the summer of 1976.

"The house was bought for us by an anonymous benefactor and we thought it would suit our purposes for at least a decade. But it is already too small. Last year we were a team of four; now we are 13 researchers and four back-up staff," says Mr Murad.

What is so unusual about the Foundation is that it is an educational research unit functioning entirely without aid from any government. A registered charity with a budget this year of £120,000, the Foundation gets its finances from philanthropic Muslims, research grants from bodies such as the Islamic Secretariat and the Islamic Solidarity Fund, a few endowments and, increasingly, sales of books.

Ultimately, the aim of the Foundation is to become self-sufficient; it is planned that the book-selling activities should play a major role in fulfilling this ambition. All the titles published are either written in-house or especially commissioned.

This autumn a book sales manager was appointed to lead a sales drive both internationally and among Britain's local education authorities, school and university and other specialist bookshops.

Titles published by the Foundation this year include *Islamic Perspectives* and *The Koran: Basic Teachings*. A Children's Islamic Library series, intended mainly for Muslim children in British schools, is now under production: four books have appeared so far and 12 more are in the pipe-line and due to come out in the next year. Among the first titles are the *Children's Book of Islam* and *Mohammed: Aspects of his Biography*.

A new departure for the Foundation is an audio-visual resources programme. A handsome wall-chart of the Muslim world has just been produced and slides, film strips and cassettes are planned for the future.

Internationally, work is going ahead, in collaboration with King Abdul Aziz University, Jeddah, on a major six-volume selection of readings in Islamic economics. This, the only such project of its kind, will be aimed at Muslim (and non-Muslim) universities world-wide. The first volume is scheduled to appear at the end of this year.

At a more theoretical level, the Foundation is establishing a documentation centre focusing on Muslim-Christian relations. As Mr Murad says: "Christianity and Islam are the world's two largest faiths. They are interacting all over the world. We think direct information and objective study will be the key to future harmonious relations."

He adds: "No such documentation is going on anywhere else in the Muslim world — though plenty of Christians are doing it. They are way ahead of us on this."

The aims of the Foundation, when it was first established by Professor Ahmad and its present assistant director, Dr M M Ahsan, were:

● to research into how to implement Islam in the modern world;

● to project the image of Islam and to improve communications between its various parts;

● to meet the educational needs of Muslims worldwide.

These remain the guiding principles of the organisation. One example of how they are being put into practice is the establishment at Leicester Polytechnic this academic year of a Fellowship in multicultural education.

The Foundation is helping to sponsor this post, which is tenable for three years and which is the only one of its type in Britain. The Fellow will be lecturing and guiding MA and PhD-level research.

For the future, Mr Murad would like to expand the "think tank" role of the Foundation, which has already inspired similar, though as yet smaller, efforts in Kenya and Nigeria. In particular, he would like to encourage more young Muslims from the developing world to spend time researching at Leicester.

An engineer by training and a graduate of Karachi and Minnesota universities, Mr Murad was born in India, and has lived and worked in Pakistan, Bangladesh, Iran and Saudi Arabia. He joined the Foundation two years ago and became director when Professor Ahmad was appointed Minister for Planning in the Pakistan Government.

Mr Murad realises the long-term success of the Foundation depends on the quality of the staff he can attract to Leicester. His philosophy on this is clear: "Our policy is to keep salaries a little below the market rate. That way we get only the most dedicated people. Our research has a spirtual dimension and is inspired by loftier motives than most western research; our commitment is to make Islam a living reality."■

The Georgian headquarters of the Islamic Foundation.

Courtesy of MIDDLE EAST EDUCATION

Appendix 1

1.   Outline of the one-day course

2.   Notes and assignments from some students who attended the course.

3.   Some basic books for the study of Islam.

Appendix 2

1.   A.R. Siddiqui: *Islamic Studies: A Select Guide to Bibliographic and Reference Material.*

2.   Some common abbreviations.

Bismillah

RESEARCH IN ISLAM - a one day seminar

Thursday 23/7/81, 10am to 5pm VENUE: Library, THE ISLAMIC FOUNDATION
Leicester.

PROGRAMME

10.00	Assemble
10.15	Welcome and introduction to the Islamic Foundation - its history, objectives and achievements.
11.00	Visiting the various units of the Islamic Foundation.
11.30	Tape-slide show as an example for audio/visual research and production.
11.45	Short break
11.50	Basics of Research (Lecture).
01.15	Wudhu.
01.30	Salatu-l-dhur.
01.45	Islamic Principles guiding Research Work (Lecture).
02.45	Assignments and exercises (Research Teams).
03.45	Reports by the Research Teams.
04.30	Evaluation of the Seminar.
05.00	Close and departure.

Appendix 1, No.2

(a)   Review of visit to Islamic Foundation on 23.7.81 - (Wan Abdul Rahman).

The idea of visiting the Islamic Foundation was suggested by a brother who was in charge of the research work which is being done as part of the programme of the summer camp. The plan was approved without objection since most brothers have heard about the Islamic Foundation but had never been there. By the grace of Allah, on 23rd July, 33 brothers and sisters managed to organise themselves to make their way to the Foundation. We arrived at about 11a.m. - about one hour later than originally planned. We were greeted by Brother Khurram Jah Murad, Brother Manazir Ahsan and Brother Ahmad von Denffer. Brother Khurram Jah, himself not very well, delivered a welcoming speech for about ten minutes. Among other things, he mentioned the importance for Muslims to realise their responsibilities and to master the language of the Qur'an. He was delighted by our visit.

Brother Manazir Ahsan introduced us to the Islamic Foundation, its work, activities, objectives and financial aspects. His talk was very informative and gave the brothers and sisters a clearer idea about the work of the Islamic Foundation. He also mentioned some problems and shortcomings of the Foundation, such as lack of manpower.

We took a 10-minute break, after which a very well-presented slide show was given about the fundamentals of Islam.

Brother Manazir returned to answer some of the questions on the Islamic Foundation. Then we performed Salatul Zuhr.

The main agenda started a bit later than planned. It was a talk on the basics of research work. This very useful talk was given by Brother Ahmad. The guidelines, hints and the technique of research are very useful, especially for us students. After that some time was spent on questions. The second talk on criteria of Islamic research had to be shortened to allow for more time for the next programme which is what I'm doing now. Brothers and sisters were divided into groups. Each group was assigned to do some work such as analysing an article, news, and review the talk.

The programme finished at 6p.m. The seven hours spent were very useful and worthwhile and most brothers and sisters agreed that it was very interesting and a chance not to be missed.

Appendix 1, No.2

(b)   Islamic Criteria for Research Work (Zaihan)

Questions are very essential for research work. Questions asked should be based on the understanding of the Qur'an, because the Qur'an is the basis of all knowledge. In order to understand the Qur'an, we have to study the Qur'an itself and to learn the language of the Qur'an. The former should not be discarded even though the latter cannot be achieved simultaneously, but should not be neglected altogether.

Justification for doing research is according to Surah 9, Ayat 122, whereby when the call of Jihad is made, some should also stay behind in order to carry on with the research work in Islam.

Two categories of doing research work:

1.   Research in Islam or Islamic studies.

2.   Research of Islamic work.

The second should be our aim as the first is restricted to specific fields of Islamic knowledge, but the second deals with Islam as a whole with relation to the problems of humanity for e.g. the Sunnat Islam is going on as it is but the laws of Allah are not practised.

Two dimensions of research in Islam:

1.   to increase our Īmān and conviction in our Islamic work.

2.   to persuade more people to listen, e.g. intellectuals, scientists, etc.

OBJECTIVE

To relate the Islamic way of life to the *status quo*, i.e. to study how the present situation in the world came about and to see the demands of Islam in their proper light. As a result of research on these two levels we can then provide the Islamic arguments in order to refute those who want to maintain the *status quo*, e.g. to be governed by man-made systems rather than the laws of Allah.

Research can also distinguish between the message of the Qur'an and Sunna in its original form and the interpretations through history. This research can expose mysticism. It can also further enhance understanding of the *tafsīr* of the Qur'an and Hadith.

Prerequisite of an Islamic research worker:

1.   *Taqwā*

2.   Have proper knowledge and competence in field of study.

3.   Have good knowledge of Islam as a whole.

4.   Be independent in thinking.

5.   Practise what you convey to others.

Methods to observe:

1.   All principles of the Qur'an and Sunna should be taken as the priority.

2.   Fuqaha/scholar should be referred to.

3.   Reason should also be taken into account but should be put in its proper place.

(2) and (3) can be interchanged in priority in certain cases.

4.   *Ijtihād* can be made out of research.

Quotation from Ibn Khaldun.

SOME BASIC BOOKS FOR THE STUDY OF ISLAM

General:

Mawdudi, Sayyid Abul Ala : *Towards Understanding Islam*, The Islamic Foundation, Leicester 1980

Mawdudi, Sayyid Abul Ala : *Fundamentals of Islam*, Islamic Publications Ltd., Lahore 1975

Abdalati, Hammudah : *Islam in Focus*, IIFSO, Kuwait 1978

Reference:

Hughes, Patrick* : *A Dictionary of Islam*, London 1895, various reprints

Freeman-Grenville,   G* : *The Muslim and Christian Calendars*, Rex Collings, London 1977

Siddiqui, Abdulhameed : *Arabic for Beginners*, Kazi, Lahore/Chicago, 1979

Rauf, Muhammad Abdul : *Arabic for English Speaking Students*, Supreme Council of Islamic Affairs, Cairo, 1972

Penrice, John* : *A Dictionary and Glossary of the Koran*, London 1873, reprint Curzon Press, London 1971

Cowan, J.M.* : *Arabic-English Dictionary*, Spoken Languages Inc., New York, 1976

Koran:

Irving, T.B., Khurshid Ahmad, M.M. Ahsan: *The Qur'an: Basic Teachings*, The Islamic Foundation, 1979

Qutb, Sayyid : *In the Shade of the Qur'an*, MWH Publishers, London 1979, Volume 30 only (incomplete)

Ali, Abdullah Yusuf : *The Holy Qur'an. Text, Translation and Commentary*, The Islamic Foundation, Leicester 1978

Pickthall, Marmaduke : *The Meanings of the Glorious Qur'an*, Taj Company, Karachi, n.d.

Mawdudi, Sayyid Abul Ala : *The Meaning of the Qur'an*, Islamic Publications Ltd., Lahore 1967-79, 8 vols. (incomplete)

Kherie, A.A. : *Index-cum-Concordance for the Holy Qur'an*, Holy Qur'an Society, Karachi 1974

Abdalbaqi, Fuad : *al-mu'jam al-mufahras li-alfaz al-quran al-karim*, al-Sha'b publisher, Cairo 1378H

Hadith:

Azami, M.M. : *Studies in Hadith Methodology and Literature*, American Trust Publications, Indianapolis 1977

Denffer, Ahmad von : *A Day with the Prophet*, The Islamic Foundation, Leicester 1979

Robson, James* : *Mishkat al-Masabih.* English translation with explanatory notes, Ashraf, Lahore 1963, 4 vols.

Siddiqui, Abdulhameed : *Sahih Muslim rendered into English*, Ashraf, Lahore 1976, 4 vols.

Khan, Muhammad Muhsin : *The Translation of the Meaning of Sahih al-Bukhari*, Hilal, Ankara 1977

Sira:

Siddiqui, Abdulhameed: *The Life of Muhammad*, Islamic Publications Ltd., Lahore 1969

Shibli Numani, A. : *Sirat al-Nabi*, translated, Pakistan Historical Society, Karachi, 1970, 2 vols.

Guillaume, Alfred* : *The Life of Muhammad*, Translation of Ibn Ishaq's *Sirat Rasul Allah*, Oxford University Press, London 1955

Fiqh:

Kamal, Abdul Aziz : *Everyday Fiqh*, Islamic Publications Ltd., Lahore 1976, 2 vols.

Howard, E.C.* : *Minhaj et-Talibin. A manual of Muhammadan law according to the school of Shafi'i, by an-Nawawi.* (Singapore 1914), reprint Law Publishing Company, Lahore 1977

History:

Arnold, T.W.* : *The Preaching of Islam. A history of the propagation of the Muslim faith*, Ashraf, Lahore 1965

Literature from the Islamic Movement:

Mawdudi, Sayyid Abul Ala : *The Process of Islamic Revolution*, Islamic Publications Ltd., Lahore 1975

Mawdudi, Sayyid Abul Ala : *The Moral Foundations of the Islamic Movement*, Islamic Publications Ltd., Lahore 1978

Mawdudi, Sayyid Abul Ala : *Islamic Movement - prerequisites for success*, Crescent, Aligarh, 1977 (also by FOSIS)

Wendell, Charles* (transl.) : *Five tracts of Hasan al-Banna*, University of Chicago Press, Chicago, 1978

Qutb, Sayyid : *Milestones*, IIFSO, Kuwait, n.d.

Islamic Research:

Khan, Qamaruddin : *The Methodology of Islamic Research*, Institute of Islamic Studies, Karachi 1973

Mawdudi, Sayyid Abul Ala : 'The Nature of Islamic Research', in : *The Criterion*, Vol. 3, No. 1, 1968, 11-24

Siddiqui, A.R. : *Islamic Studies : A select guide to bibliographical and reference material*, The Islamic Foundation, Leicester 1979

Research:

Hoffmann, Ann* : *Research. A Handbook for Writers and Journalists*, Adam, Charles and Black, London 1979

Maddox, Harry* : *How to study*, Pan Books, London 1967

*   non-Muslim author or translator

Appendix No. 2, 1.

ISLAMIC STUDIES : A SELECT
GUIDE TO BIBLIOGRAPHIC AND
REFERENCE MATERIAL[1]

by

A.R. Siddiqui[2]

---

1.   The original version was previously published as 'Seminar Papers No.1' by The Islamic Foundation, Leicester, 1979. This is a revised and updated version. I am grateful to Brother A.R. Siddiqui for his kind permission to include his valuable guide in my handbook.

2.   The author graduated in Economics and Politics from the University of Bombay and has a law degree from the same University. He completed his post-graduate course in librarianship at North West Polytechnic, London and was elected to the Associateship of the Library Association. He is working as a Reference Librarian for Social Sciences, Law and Official Publications at the University of Leicester.

TABLE OF CONTENTS

Introduction

1.   Guides to Bibliographic Resources in the Field

    .1   Bibliographies

    .2   Guides to Reference Books

    .3   General Handbooks

    .31   Specialised Handbooks

2.   Books

    .1   Current National and Comprehensive Bibliographies

    .2   Library Catalogues

    .3   Current Specialised Bibliographies

    .4   Translations

3.   Periodical Articles

    .1   General

    .2   Specialised

    .3   Current Survey of Events

    .4   Current Awareness

    .5   Other Disciplines

4.   <u>Theses</u>

    .1   Great Britain

    .2   United States

5.   <u>Reference Books</u>

    .1   Dictionaries and Encyclopaedias

    .2   Directories and Yearbooks

    .3   Atlases

    .4   Biographies

INTRODUCTION

Literature search means searching the literature for relevant information as opposed to browsing and discovering materials by serendipity. The need for a systematic approach is becoming increasingly important as the world output of literature is approaching what is often called 'information explosion'. Hence to avoid duplication of research, it is more sensible to do some basic literature search first. An enormous amount of time can be saved by taking the trouble to search existing bibliographies. It will be a waste of time and energy to compile a bibliography or conduct a 'subject search' if someone has already done the work and published it.

In this guide, I have cited works published in the English language only. Reasons for excluding other languages are threefold:

1.   'Islamic Studies' is such a vast subject that compilation of a comprehensive guide would make this difficult task beyond my capability.

2.   This guide is primarily aimed at students who are not familiar with 'Islamic languages'.

3.   I want to dispel an erroneous belief about the lack of material available in English on Islam. I know that not all publications may be suitable for clear understanding of Islamic faith and that many are biased and prejudiced. But a discriminating reader should be able to evaluate them and form his own judgement. One should not forget that quite a few books written by 'Muslims' in 'Islamic languages' also suffer from these maladies. Translations from Arabic, Persian, Turkish and Urdu of many basic books into English, to some extent overcome the disadvantage of not knowing the original sources.

Even with this self-imposed restriction, I have to be selective and I have to leave out many useful sources of reference. Insha Allah, I will try to cover some of the more specialised works of reference in regional guides or topical guides, if resources and time become available for this arduous but very pleasant and satisfying job.

October, 1978   A.R. Siddiqui

ISLAMIC STUDIES - A SELECT GUIDE TO BIBLIOGRAPHIC AND REFERENCE MATERIAL

1. ## Guides to Bibliographic Resources in the Field

1.1 ### Bibliographies

BESTERMAN, Theodore

A World Bibliography of Bibliographies 4th ed.

Lausanne : Societas Bibliographica, 1965-66. 5 vols.

A classified bibliography of separately published bibliographies of books. 117,000 items grouped under 16,000 headings and sub-headings.

TOOMEY, Alice F.

A World Bibliography of Bibliographies, 1964-1974

Totowa : Rowman and Littlefield, 1977. 2 vols.

A decennial supplement to Besterman.

BIBLIOGRAPHIC INDEX, New York : H.W. Wilson, 1937-

Published three times a year. Third part cumulates the previous two issues to form an annual, then there are five-year cumulations. Published bibliographies are arranged under specific subject headings.

BARROW, John Graves

A Bibliography of Bibliographies in Religion

Ann Arbor : Edward Bros., 1955

Primarily Christian but with a brief section on non-Christian religions. Brief annotations and author index.

GEDDES, Charles L.

An Analytical Guide to the Bibliographies on Islam, Muhammad and the Qur'an, Denver, Colo.: American Institute of Islamic Studies, 1973.

An annotated bibliography of more than 200 bibliographies published in monographic forms or as articles in learned journals. Certain library catalogues are also included. Arranged alphabetically by authors with a subject index. Includes material in Arabic, Persian, Turkish as well as European languages.

GEDDES, Charles L.

An Analytical Guide to the Bibliographies on the Arab Fertile Crescent. Denver : American Institute of Islamic Studies, 1975.

A comprehensive annotated bibliography of bibliographies on Iraq, Jordan, Lebanon and Syria listing also many general bibliographies on the Near and Middle East, with a separate section on the Arab-Israeli conflict. Titles in other foreign languages e.g. Arabic, Russian and French are included.

1.2   Guides to Reference Books

SHEEHY, E.P.

Guide to Reference Books, 9th ed.   Chicago : American Library Association, 1976.

Lists bibliographic and reference sources with critical and descriptive notes. Systematic arrangement, items BB341-350 and DE20-47 on Islam. Author and title indexes.

WALFORD, A.J.

Guide to Reference Material, 3rd ed. London: Library Association, 1975. 3 vols.

About 3,000 reference books arranged by Universal Decimal Classification. Vol.2 contains reference works on religions. Class 97 is Islam.

1.3 General Handbooks

ADAMS, Charles Joseph.

A Reader's Guide to the Great Religions, 2nd ed.
New York: Free Press, 1977.

A collection of bibliographic essays by specialists on the world's principal religions. Contribution on Islam by Professor Adams of McGill University runs to 50 pages with appendices on reference books and periodicals.

MITROS, Joseph F.

Religions : A Select Classified Bibliography
New York : Learned Publications, 1973.

A classified bibliography intended for research students. Covers all major religions. Titles mainly in English, but foreign works are also included.

WALSH, Michael J. (compiler)

Religious Bibliographies in Serial Literature : a guide
London : Mansell, 1981.

Produced under the auspices of the Association of British Theological and Philosophical Libraries. Very well annotated guide to

178 bibliographical tools with comprehensive subject index.

1.31 Specialised Handbooks

AMERICAN INSTITUTE OF ISLAMIC STUDIES

Islam in Paperback. Denver : The Institute, 1969.

A useful listing of all U.S. and British paperbacks, with annotations under broad subject headings. Lacks author and title indexes. Now becoming out of date.

ATIYEH, George H.

The Contemporary Middle East, 1948-1973 : a selected and annotated bibliography. Boston : G.K. Hall, 1975.

Lists nearly 6,500 books and periodical articles with brief annotations. Very comprehensive coverage for this period. Contains author and subject indexes.

BACHARACH, J.L.

A Near East Studies Handbook, rev. ed.

Seattle : University of Washington Press, 1977.

Very useful handbook. Includes dynasties, rulers, geneology and historical atlas. Chronological list meticulously compiled.

BIRNBAUM, E.

Books on Asia from the Near East to the Far East : A Guide
for the General Reader.   Toronto : University of Toronto Press,
1971.

Chapter on Islamic Literature is well annotated.

ETTINGHAUSEN, Richard

A selected and Annotated Bibliography of Books and
Periodicals in Western Languages dealing with the Near East
and Middle East with special emphasis on medieval and modern
times. Washington : The Middle East Institute, 1954.

General bibliography with helpful annotations. Now very much
out of date.

HOPEWOOD, Derek and GRIMWOOD-JONES, Diana

Middle East and Islam : A Bibliographical Introduction,
rev. ed. Zug, Switzerland: Inter Documentation, 1979.

Sections on Islamic history, law, political science by scholars
and librarians. Presentation uneven.

LITTLEFIELD, David W.

The Islamic Near East and North Africa : an annotated guide to books in English for non-specialists. Littleton, Colo. : Libraries Unlimited, 1977.

A good guide to 'standard' works available with extensive critical notes. Lists 1,166 works under broad subject headings and countries. Author, title and subject indexes. Appendices provide suitability of each item to different types of libraries and categories of readers.

PEARSON, J.D. (ed.)

Arab Islamic Bibliography. Hassocks : Harvester Press, 1977.

Based on GABRIELL's *Manuale di bibliografia Musulmana* published in 1916 in Italian. Contributors attempt to bring this work up to date. Contains series of bibliographical essays on each topic listing bibliography, reference books, periodicals and manuscripts.

PEARSON, J.D.

Oriental and Asian Bibliography : An Introduction with some Reference to Africa. London : Crosby Lockwood, 1966.

Guide to Oriental studies in Europe, lists organisations and libraries, specialists collections manuscripts, collections in the field.

SAINT JOSEPH'S UNIVERSITY. Centre for the Study of the Modern Arab World.

Arab Culture and Society in Change. Beirut : Dar El-Mashreq, 1973.

Contains references to nearly 5,000 books and articles on culture and change in the Middle East and North Africa. Systematically arranged with author, regions and subject indexes.

SAUVAGET, J.

Introduction to the History of the Muslim East : A Bibliographical Guide, based on the 2nd ed. by C. Cohen. Berkeley : University of California Press, 1965.

Translation and revised edition of Cohen's 1961 edition. Divided into 3 parts: 1. Sources of Muslim history. 2. Tools of research. 3. Historical bibliography.

ZUWIYYA, Jalal

The Near East - South West Asia and North Africa : A Bibliographic Study.   Metuchen : Scarecrow Press, 1973.

Based on the holdings of the State University of New York Library listing 3,600 items. Author and title indexes.

2.   Books

2.1   Current National and Comprehensive Bibliographies

BRITISH NATIONAL BIBLIOGRAPHY

London : Council of the BNB, 1950 -

Weekly with 3 cumulations a year, an annual volume and 5 year cumulations. All books with British imprint included. Main sections classified by Dewey. Author/title and subject indexes.

Cumulative Book Index

New York : H.W. Wilson, 1928 -

Monthly, cumulating at intervals. Covers all publications in English.
One alphabetical sequence of entries under author, title and subject.

Religious Books and Series in Print 1978-79.

New York : R.R. Bowker, 1979.

Entries are extracted from *Books in Print* and *Subject Guide to Books
in Print*. There are author, title and subject indexes. Two additional
useful indexes are for the Sacred Works and Serial publications.

Subject Index to Books in Print

New York : Bowker, 1966 -

Annual publication of books available arranged under specific subject
headings.

2.2 Library Catalogues

BRITISH LIBRARY, Department of Printed Books.

Subject Index of Modern Works. London : B.L., 1881-

Better known as British Museum Library. Excellent for early books.
Latest cumulation for 1956-60.

NATIONAL UNION CATALOG

Books : Subjects. New York : Rowman & Littlefield, 1950 -

Invaluable tool because of the immensity of the collection and full bibliographical description. Latest cumulation for 1970-74. There are annual cumulations from 1975 onwards.

London Bibliography of the Social Sciences

London : L.S.E., 1931-32.

Most extensive bibliography of works in the social sciences. Lists by subject, holdings of several London Libraries. Latest cumulation up to 1981.

UNIVERSITY OF CHICAGO, Oriental Institute.

Catalog of the Oriental Institute Library. Boston : G.K. Hall, 1970. 16 vols. First supplement 1977 - 1 vol.

Lists over 50,000 books on the Near East.

UNIVERSITY OF LONDON, School of Oriental and African Studies.

Library Catalogue. Boston : G.K. Hall, 1963. 28 vols.
First supplement 1968 - 16 volumes, second supplement 1973 - 16 volumes, third supplement 1979 - 19 volumes.

Contains more than 14 million cards. A considerable number of analytical entries to be found, drawn from periodicals.

MCGILL UNIVERSITY, Institute of Islamic Studies.

The Library Catalog.   Boston : G.K. Hall, 1977.

Lists 75,000 vols. and the largest collection of periodicals on Islam. Includes 500 reels of microfilms of rare books and manuscripts.

MCGILL UNIVERSITY. Institute of Islamic Studies.

Periodica Islamica, a check-list of serials available at McGill Islamics Library; compiled by Muzaffar Ali.

Montreal : The Institute, 1973.

2.3   Current Specialised Bibliographies

International Bibliography of the History of Religions

Leiden : E.J. Brill, V.1-23. 1954-1979.

Section on Islam. Lists books and articles published during the year. Classified arrangement. No author index until 1958/59. No longer published. Replaced by *Science of Religion* (see under section 3.2)

LIBRARY OF CONGRESS

Accession List : Middle East.   Cairo : L.C., V.1 - 1963-

Similar lists produced for other countries, e.g. Pakistan, India, Israel, etc.

The Muslim World Book Review. Leicester : Islamic Foundation,
Vol.1 -   1980 -

Quarterly. Some in-depth reviews, others short introductions and
select bibliographies on specific topics.

New Books Quarterly on Islam and the Muslim World
London : Islamic Council of Europe. Vol.1 -   1981 -

Lists new and forthcoming English publications though other languages are also included from time to time.

2.4   Translations

Index Translationum : International Bibliography of Translations.
Paris : UNESCO, N.J. Vol.1 - 1948.

Entries under countries then arranged by Universal Decimal Classification. Index of authors.

FARRAR, C.P. and EVANS, A.P.

Bibliography of English Translations from Medieval Sources.
New York : Columbia U.P., 1946.

Lists translations of many Islamic works published as monographs
or periodical articles.

FERGUSON, M.A.H.

Bibliography of English Translations from Medieval Sources
1943-1967. New York : Columbia U.P., 1974.

This supplements the above work and brings it up to date.

3.   Periodical Articles

3.1   General

Arts & Humanities Citation Index

Philadelphia; Institute for Scientific Information, 1976 -

The rationale of citation indexing is that authors references reflect
subject relationship to works cited. Avoids semantic difficulties in
choosing right indexing terms. Covers over 1,000 journals.

British Humanities Index

London : Library Association 1962 -

Quarterly subject index with annual cumulations of about 300 British
periodicals and newspapers. Separate author index.

Humanities Index
New York : H.W. Wilson, 1974 -

Indexes about 200 mostly American and British journals. Citations to
book reviews are also included.

Social Sciences Index

New York : H.W. Wilson, 1974 -

Indexes cover 260 journals. Counterpart of *Humanities Index*.
Between 1964 and 1973 published as *Social Sciences and Humanities
Index* and from 1916 to 1963 as *International Index*.

Social Science Citation Index

Philadelphia : Institute for Scientific Information, 1966 -

Covers over 4,000 journals.

3.2   Specialised

Index Islamicus : a catalogue of articles on Islamic subjects
in periodicals and other collective volumes, 1906-1955.

Cambridge : Heffer, and London : Mansell.

5 yearly cumulations 1956-60; 1961-65; 1966-70; 1971-75 so far
published. 1976-80 is under preparation. Quarterly from 1977.
Classified guide to periodical literature with an author index. Fests-
chriften are also analysed. From 1977 books are also indexed. Entries
arranged systematically.

LJUNGGREN, F.

The Arab World Index : an international guide to periodical
literature in the Social Sciences and Humanities in the Contemporary Arab World, 1960-64. Cairo : American University, 1967.

Religious Index One : Periodicals

Chicago : American Theological Library Association, Vol.1 -
1949/52 -

Semi-annual; every fourth issue a bound cumulation for two years.
Indexes over 200 periodicals mainly published in Western countries.
Includes book reviews as well. Vols. 1-12 (1949/52 - 1975/76) pub-
lished under the title *Index to Religious Periodical Literature.*

Religion Index Two : Multi-Author Works

Chicago : American Theological Library Association, Vol.1 -
1976 -

Annual. Supplements the preceding work and fills a gap by indexing
a form of publication otherwise difficult to retrieve.

Religious and Theological Abstracts

Youngtown, Ohio : Theological Publ., 1958 -

Quarterly with annual cumulations. A non-sectarian approach in
presenting brief abstracts in English of select Christian, Jewish and
Islamic journals in various languages.

Science of Religion Bulletin : Abstracts and Index of recent
articles.   Amsterdam: Institute for the Study of Religion,

Free University, 1974 -   Quarterly.

Indexes about 18 periodicals on Islam in English, French and German.

3.3   Current Survey of Events

Annual Register of World Events

London : Longman 1758 -   Annual.

Global in scope but British affairs get fullest treatment. Political
events in each country by specialists. Separate sections on religion,
science, law, economics, arts and literature. Contains important
documents, maps and obituaries.

Keesing's Contemporary Archives : Weekly diary of world events
with Index. London : Keesing's, 1931 -

Loose-leaf digest of newspapers. Authoritative and well documented
source of reference. Very well indexed.

New York Times Index
N.Y. Times 1913 -

The Times

Index to The Times

Palmer's 1790-1922

Official 1923-

3.4   Current Awareness

Current Contents : Arts and Humanities. Philadelphia : Institute
for Scientific Information, 1979 -

Reproduces tables of contents of about 1,000 journals. Articles copying service available. Useful for keeping abreast of current output of periodical literature.

3.5   Other Disciplines

International Bibliography of Social Sciences 1952 -

Separate volumes for Sociology, Economics, Political Science and Social and Cultural Anthropology.

International Political Science Abstracts 1952 -

Historical Abstracts 1955 -

Sociological Abstracts 1952 -

4.   THESES

4.1   Great Britain

ASLIB

Index to theses accepted for higher degrees in the universities of Great Britain and Ireland.

London : Aslib, Vol.1 -   1950/51-   Annual.

Classified arrangement of theses by very broad subject headings. Author and subject indexes.

Retrospective Index to Theses of Great Britain and Ireland 1716-1950.

Santa Barbara : American Bibliographical Centre - Clio Press, Vol.1 Social Sciences and Humanities, 1975.

Very well indexed collection of theses. Supplements Aslib.

BLOOMFIELD, B.D.

Theses on Asia accepted by universities in the United Kingdom and Ireland,1877-1964.London : Frank Cass, 1967.

Regional grouping of theses subdivided by subjects e.g. economics, international relations, law, politics, religion and history. Regularly updated in the *Bulletin of the British Association of Orientalists*.

INSTITUTE OF RELIGION AND THEOLOGY OF GREAT BRITAIN AND IRELAND Current Research. 5th ed.

Sunderland : The Institute, 1980 + 1981 supplement.

Entries are arranged under word subject headings. No author index.

UNIVERSITY OF DURHAM, Centre for Middle Eastern and Islamic Studies.

Current British Research in Middle Eastern Studies.

Durham University, 1971.

Alphabetical list of researchers followed by broad subject index, e.g. anthropology, philosophy and religion, language and literature. There is a regional index as well. Latest ed. No.3, 1977.

4.2   United States

SELIM, G.S.

American doctoral dissertations on the Arab World 1883-1968.
Washington : Library of Congress, 1970.

About 1,000 items are listed. Includes a subject index.

Dissertation Abstracts International

Ann Arbor : Univ. Microfilms, 1952 -

Title misleading as mostly American and Canadian theses are
listed. Coverage expanded to include British, Australian and European theses as well. *Section A* Humanities and Social Sciences,
Section B Science and Engineering, *Section C* European 1976 -
. Monthly compilation of doctoral dissertations, with author
and subject indexes. Catalogues containing a selection of dissertations on various topics are also available on request.

5.   Reference books

5.1   Dictionaries and Encyclopaedias

Encyclopaedia of Islam

Leiden : Brill, 1915 - 38.   4 vols. + suppl.

2nd ed.   1960 -

Works of high scholarship and authority containing signed articles on all aspects of Islamic life, thought and history. Indispensible work of reference. Second edition in progress; issued in fascicules. 4 vols. up to letter K so far published. A supplement and an index to volumes 1-3 have appeared.

HUGHES, T.P.

A dictionary of Islam. London : W.H. Allen, 1895.

Still useful for short definitions.

RONART, S. and RONART, N.

Concise Encyclopaedia of Arabic Civilisation

Amsterdam : Djambatan, 1959-66. 2 vols.

Vol. 1 The Arab East. Vol. 2 The Arab West.

A handy if rather uneven short reference book on many aspects of Muslim civilisation.

Shorter Encyclopaedia of Islam

Leiden : Brill, 1953.

Articles on the religion and law taken from the 1st ed. with some additions and updating. There is a useful register of subjects which indexes the entries under English language headings.

FREEMAN-GRENVILLE, G.S.P.

The Muslim and Christian Calendars

London : Oxford U.P., 1963.

Tables for the conversion of Muslim and Christian dates from the Hijra to the year 2000. Also lists important festivals of both religions.

5.2   Directories and Yearbooks

LJUNGGREN, F. and GEDDES, C.L.

An International directory of institutes and societies interested in the Middle East

Amsterdam : Djambatan, 1962.

Middle East and North Africa : A Survey and Directory.

London : Europa, 1948 -

Gives brief historical introduction to each country in the region - sections on economics, politics, education, law, etc. Statistical tables are very useful. Published every two years.

RUDKIN, Anthony and BUTCHER, Irene

A Book world directory of the Arab Countries, Turkey and Iran.

London : Mansell, 1981.

Arranged in country sections, provides information on libraries, book-sellers, commercial and institutional publishers, newspapers and periodical publications.

World Muslim Gazetteer
Karachi : Umma Publishing House, 1975.

Arranged in four parts. Part I: Independent Muslim countries.
Part 2: Muslim countries/areas under non-Muslim control. Part 3:
Organisations in Muslim world, e.g. Arab League, Muslim Conference
etc. Part 4: Muslim world in figures.

5.3   ATLASES

Atlas of the Arab World and the Middle East

London : Macmillan, 1960.

Contains an introduction by Professor G.F. Beckingham.

HAZARD, H.W.

Atlas of Islamic History. 3rd ed.

Princeton U.P., 1954.

Includes conversion tables of Christian and Muslim dates and index
of place names.

ROBINSON, Francis

Atlas of the Islamic World Since 1500. Oxford : Phaidon Press,
1982.

ROULVINK, R.

Historical Atlas of the Muslim Peoples

Amsterdam : Djambatan, 1957.

Very clear and well produced maps.

5.4   Biographies

BEALE, T.W.

An Oriental Biographical Dictionary. London :   1894, repr.

New York : Kraus Reprints, 1965.

Very brief biographical notes. Indexing of names is very
haphazard.

IBN KHALLIKAN

Kitab Wafayat al-a'yan.   London : Allen & Co., 1843-71.

Translated by de Slane in 4 vols. Compiled in 6th century of Hijra.
Another edition translated by S. Moinul Haq is published by the
Pakistan Historical Society.

al-NADIM

The Fihrist.   New York : Columbia U.P., 1970.

Encyclopaedic work of bio-bibliographical nature depicting cultural
achievements of Muslims in 4th century A.H.

Who's Who in the Arab World

Beirut : Publitec Publication, 1965/66 -

A comprehensive survey of 15 Arab countries giving details of their
economics and social structure. Other part of the book contains biographical notes on 3,000 leading personalities in the Arab world.

BOSWORTH, C.E.

The Islamic Dynasties.   Edinburgh U.P., 1967.

Lists rulers of 82 Islamic dynasties in all parts of the world, from beginning of Islam to present day. Each dynasty preceded by a brief historical note.

LANE-POOLE, S.

The Muhammadan Dynasties.   London : A. Constable & Co., 1894.

Provides chronological and geneological tables with historical intro-ductions for each dynasty.

Appendix No.2, 2.

Some Common Abbreviations

cf.	compare
Ch.	chapter
ed.	edited by, editor
e.g.	for example
et. al.	and others
etc.	and so forth
f., ff.	following page, following pages
ibid.	in the same place
i.e.	that is
infra	below
l., ll	line, lines
loc. cit.	in the cited place
MS, MSS	manuscript, manuscripts
n.	note
n.d.	no date
N.B.	please note
op. cit.	in the work cited
p., pp.	page, pages

passim	here and there
rev.	revised
sic	thus (indicating a mistake reproduced and not corrected)
supra	above
tr.	translated by, translator
vide	see
V., vol.	volume